GW00585806

9 22000001 43 717

Your Body and You

LOOKING AFTER YOUR BODY

By Anita Ganeri

Illustrated by Vera Popova

W

FRANKLIN WATTS

LONDON•SYDNEY

First published by The Watts Publishing Group in 2021

HB ISBN 978 1 4451 7536 2
PB ISBN 978 1 4451 7537 9

Credits
Series editor: Julia Bird
Illustrator: Vera Popova
Packaged by: Collaborate

Franklin Watts
An imprint of
Hachette Children's Group
Part of The Watts Publishing Group
Carmelite House
50 Victoria Embankment
London EC4Y 0DZ

An Hachette UK Company
www.hachette.co.uk
www.franklinwatts.co.uk
Printed in Dubai

Note to parents and teachers: every effort has been made by the Publishers to ensure websites are suitable for children, that they are of the highest educational value, and that they contain no inappropriate or offensive material. However, because of the nature of the Internet, it is impossible to guarantee that the contents of these sites will not be altered. We strongly advise that Internet access is supervised by a responsible adult.

CONTENTS

BODY CARE

Think of everything you do during a day. From the time you get up, you're busy.

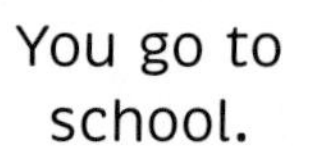

You go to school.

You play sport.

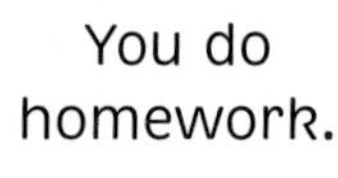

You do homework.

At the weekend, you're probably just as busy.

You might go cycling.

You might dance in a show.

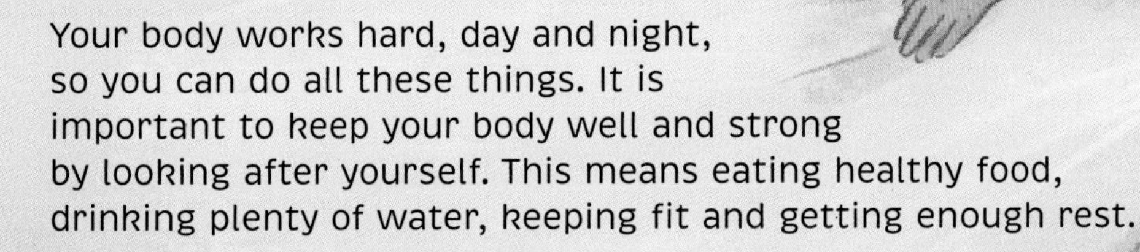

Your body works hard, day and night, so you can do all these things. It is important to keep your body well and strong by looking after yourself. This means eating healthy food, drinking plenty of water, keeping fit and getting enough rest.

GOOD FOOD

Your busy body uses up lots of energy. Energy comes from the food you eat.

As you grow up, your body changes. This uses up more energy, and you probably feel hungry a lot of the time! This tells you your body needs refuelling, so what are the best things to eat?

On this plate you can get an idea of how much of each kind of food you should eat.

Fruit and vegetables

Protein

To keep active and healthy, a balanced diet is best. This means eating a mixture of different kinds of food. Eat lots of fruit and vegetables and carbohydrates, like pasta or rice. Keep sweet or fatty goods for treats.

TOP TIP

Next time you need a quick snack, grab an apple or some plain popcorn. They're healthier than chocolate or crisps, and just as tasty.

FEELING THIRSTY

Your body needs plenty of water to keep it healthy.

If you don't drink enough, your body can't work properly and you may start feeling ill. Keep a water bottle handy at home or at school. Don't forget to top it up during the day.

Water is great to drink on its own, or you can mix it with your favourite sugar-free squash.

Semi-skimmed milk is also good to drink. It's packed with calcium, which helps make your bones and teeth strong.

It's okay to have fruit juice and fizzy drinks sometimes, but not every day. They're full of sugar and acid, which can rot your teeth. It's best to drink them with a meal. This does less harm to your teeth.

Lots of fruit and vegetables also contain water, along with vital nutrients.

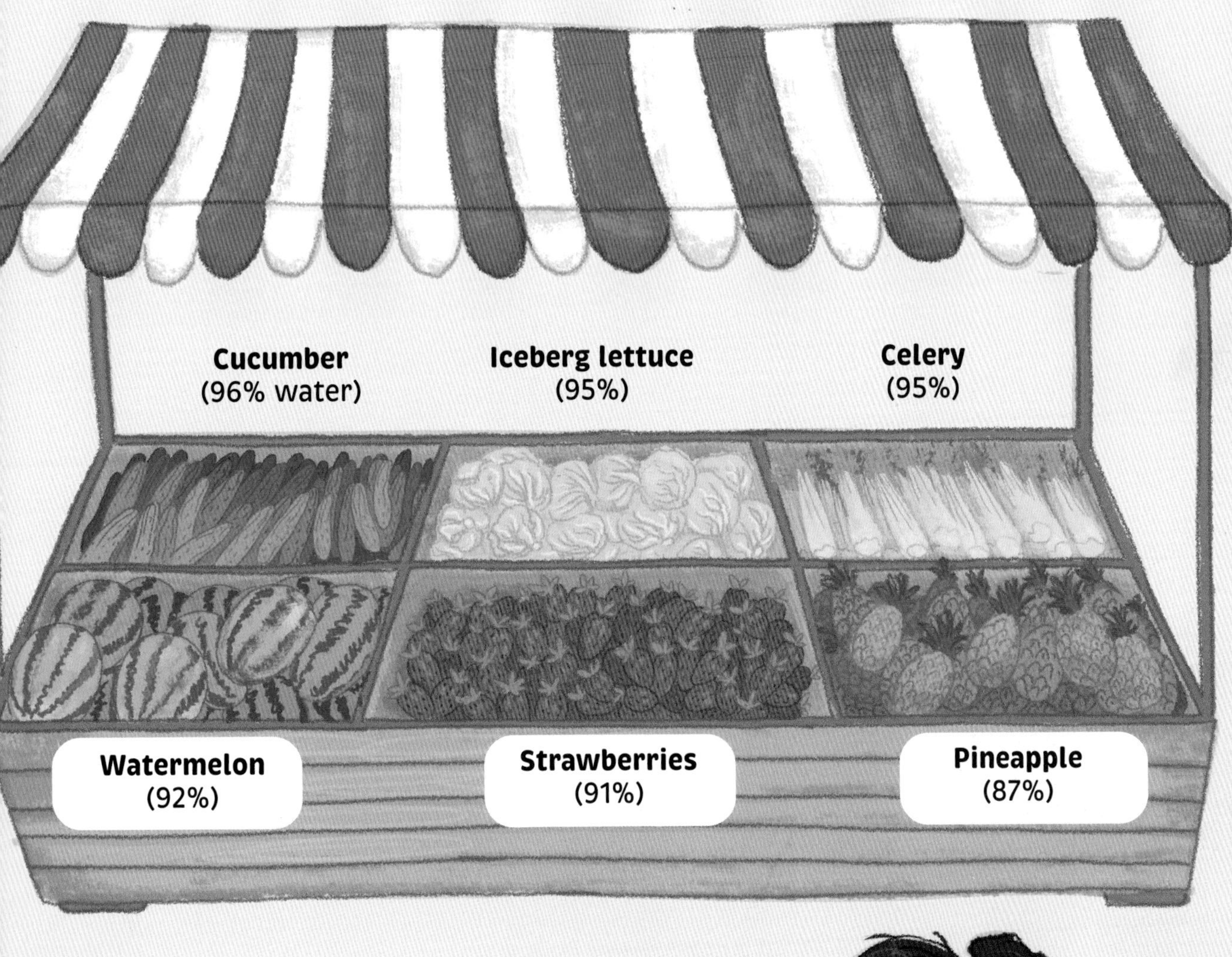

TOP TIP

Try to drink around 5–6 glasses of water a day. You'll need to drink more if the weather's warm or if you're doing sport.

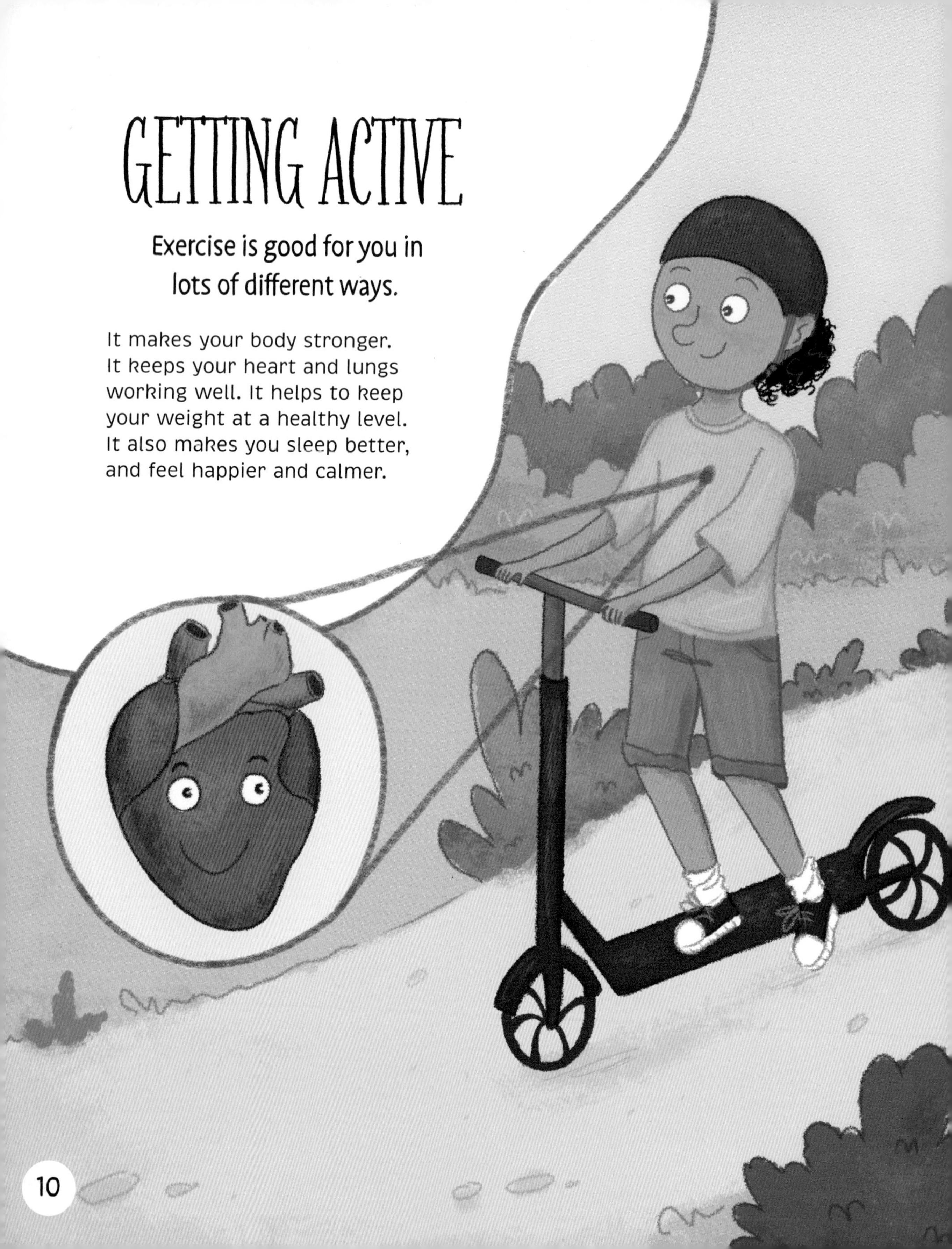

GETTING ACTIVE

Exercise is good for you in lots of different ways.

It makes your body stronger. It keeps your heart and lungs working well. It helps to keep your weight at a healthy level. It also makes you sleep better, and feel happier and calmer.

But what if you don't enjoy PE, or feel too tired to exercise when you come home from school? The trick is to find something you enjoy. That way, you're more likely to stick to it. There are lots of ideas to try on the next two pages. You can try things like walking, scootering or cycling to school, taking the dog for a walk or dancing to your favourite music with a friend.

Try to do some exercise most days, even if you don't feel like it. When you get used to it, you'll find it easier to keep going. You don't have to do it all in one go. You can break it up into short chunks to do at different times of the day.

ON THE MOVE

Are you ready to get moving? You don't have to be super-sporty. Try out different activities until you find one you really like.

Here are some ideas. With any new exercise, start off gently and build up slowly. This will stop you getting injured. And don't forget to have fun!

TOP TIP

Teaming up with a fitness buddy will help you stick with exercise. If one of you is feeling tired or fed up, the other can keep you both going.

SLEEP TIGHT

After a busy day, your body needs a break. It needs a good night's sleep. Sleep gives your body a chance to recharge, ready for the next day.

If you don't get enough sleep, you might ...

... feel tired and grumpy

... have trouble thinking clearly

...struggle to stay awake in lessons.

You might also ...

... find it hard to remember things

... get ill more often

... not grow as much as you should.

Sleep is important for staying healthy, learning and feeling good. But what happens if you have a hard time nodding off at night? Here are some top sleep tips.

1. Try to go to bed at the same time every night.
2. Have a warm bath, or read a book to relax.
3. Don't do any exercise just before bedtime.
4. Make your bedroom a calm and relaxing space.
5. Turn off any tech at least an hour before going to bed.
6. Close your eyes and count backwards from 100, 99, 98, 97 ...

Some people need more sleep than others. Between the ages of 5 and 12, try to get around 10–11 hours' sleep a night.

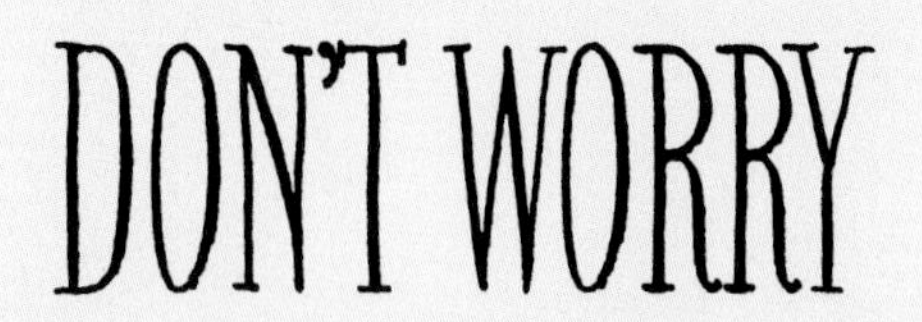

DON'T WORRY

You might find it hard to fall asleep if you're worried about something.

Worries can seem worse at night, and go around and around in your mind. It's easy for them to seem bigger and worse than they really are.

Everyone feels worried, scared or sad sometimes. It's all part of being human. You might have a test coming up at school. You might have fallen out with your best friend. Your family pet might be ill. Looking after your feelings is just as important as looking after your body.

It's important to tell someone if you're feeling down. Don't keep it to yourself. Talk to your mum, dad or another trusted adult. At school, you can speak to your teacher or the school nurse. Telling someone will make you feel better, and help you find ways of coping with your worries.

STRESS BUSTING

There are lots of things you can do to help yourself feel happier and more positive. Then you can get on with enjoying life!

Do things you enjoy, like seeing your friends.

Make sure that you get enough sleep.

Get plenty of exercise, especially outdoors.

Eat a healthy diet and drink lots of water.

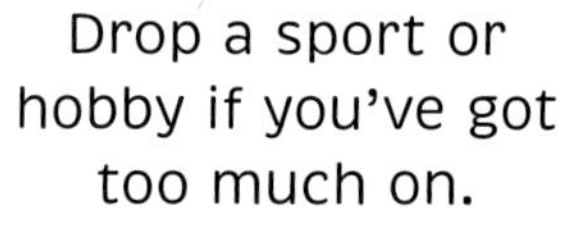

Drop a sport or hobby if you've got too much on.

Think about the good stuff, no matter how small.

Remember, it's not just you. Everyone feels down sometimes.

Make a list of things that are worrying you.

Now make a list of things you like about your life.

One way to feel calm is to focus on your breathing. It takes a bit of practice, but it really works.

1. Find a place where you can sit quietly.
2. Breathe in deeply, through your nose.
3. Breathe from your tummy, not your chest.
4. Breathe out slowly, through your mouth.
5. Wait a few seconds, then try it again.

KEEPING CLEAN

Hate the idea of having a shower? Can't be bothered to hop in the bath? Don't worry – you're not alone!

But keeping your body clean will help you feel better and stay healthier. It's a good idea to have a wash every day. This is especially important if you've been running around with friends or playing sport.

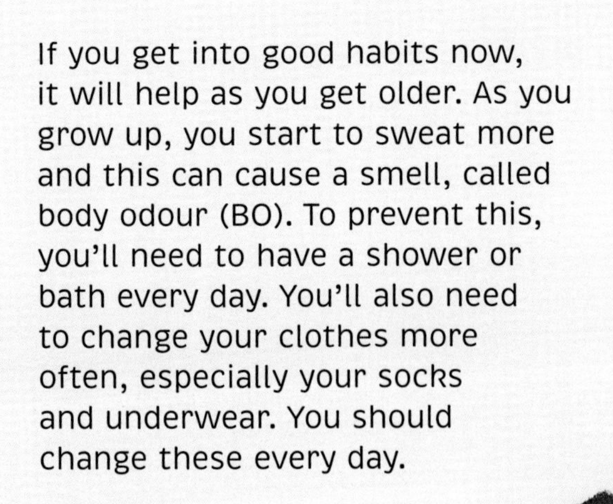

If you get into good habits now, it will help as you get older. As you grow up, you start to sweat more and this can cause a smell, called body odour (BO). To prevent this, you'll need to have a shower or bath every day. You'll also need to change your clothes more often, especially your socks and underwear. You should change these every day.

DID YOU KNOW?

Your skin and hair will probably get greasier as you grow up. This is because of oil being made in your skin. You might need to wash your face and hair more often.

HEALTHY TEETH

Are your parents always reminding you to brush your teeth? It's good advice.

Healthy teeth help you to eat, speak and smile. But sugar and acid in your food can harm your teeth and gums. You might end up with painful toothache or even have to have a tooth taken out.

To keep your teeth healthy, brush them twice a day. Squeeze a pea-sized blob of toothpaste onto your toothbrush. Brush your teeth for at least two minutes each time (some electric toothbrushes can time this for you). Make sure that you brush all your teeth, not just the ones at the front. Spit out the toothpaste - don't swallow it.

Don't miss regular check-ups at the dentist - you should go twice a year. The dentist will check your teeth and gums. They will also tell you the best way to brush, and help keep your teeth sparkling white and clean.

STAYING WELL

You've been doing a brilliant job of looking after your body. But things can still go wrong sometimes.

Here are some of the most common illnesses you might get, and what they do to your body.

COLD

Caused by: cold viruses

Symptoms: runny nose; sneezing; stuffy nose; watery eyes; cough; feeling tired

CHICKENPOX

Caused by: the chickenpox virus

Symptoms: fever; rash of itchy spots; runny nose; tummy ache

If you're feeling ill, make sure you talk to your mum or dad. Many illnesses are easy to treat at home, and will clear up quickly. For more serious problems, your parents might need to take you to see the doctor.

TUMMY BUG

Caused by: a virus or bacteria in food

Symptoms: being sick; diarrhoea; tummy ache; fever

TONSILLITIS

Caused by: a virus or bacteria

Symptoms: sore throat; fever; headache; pain when swallowing

WASH YOUR HANDS!

Many illnesses are caused by bacteria or viruses. We also call them germs.

A favourite place for germs to be is on your hands. Whenever you touch things, germs get onto your hands. If you touch your eyes, nose and mouth afterwards, the germs can get into your body and make you ill.

You can also pass germs onto other people, and they can become ill, too. The best way to stop this happening is to wash your hands often during the day.

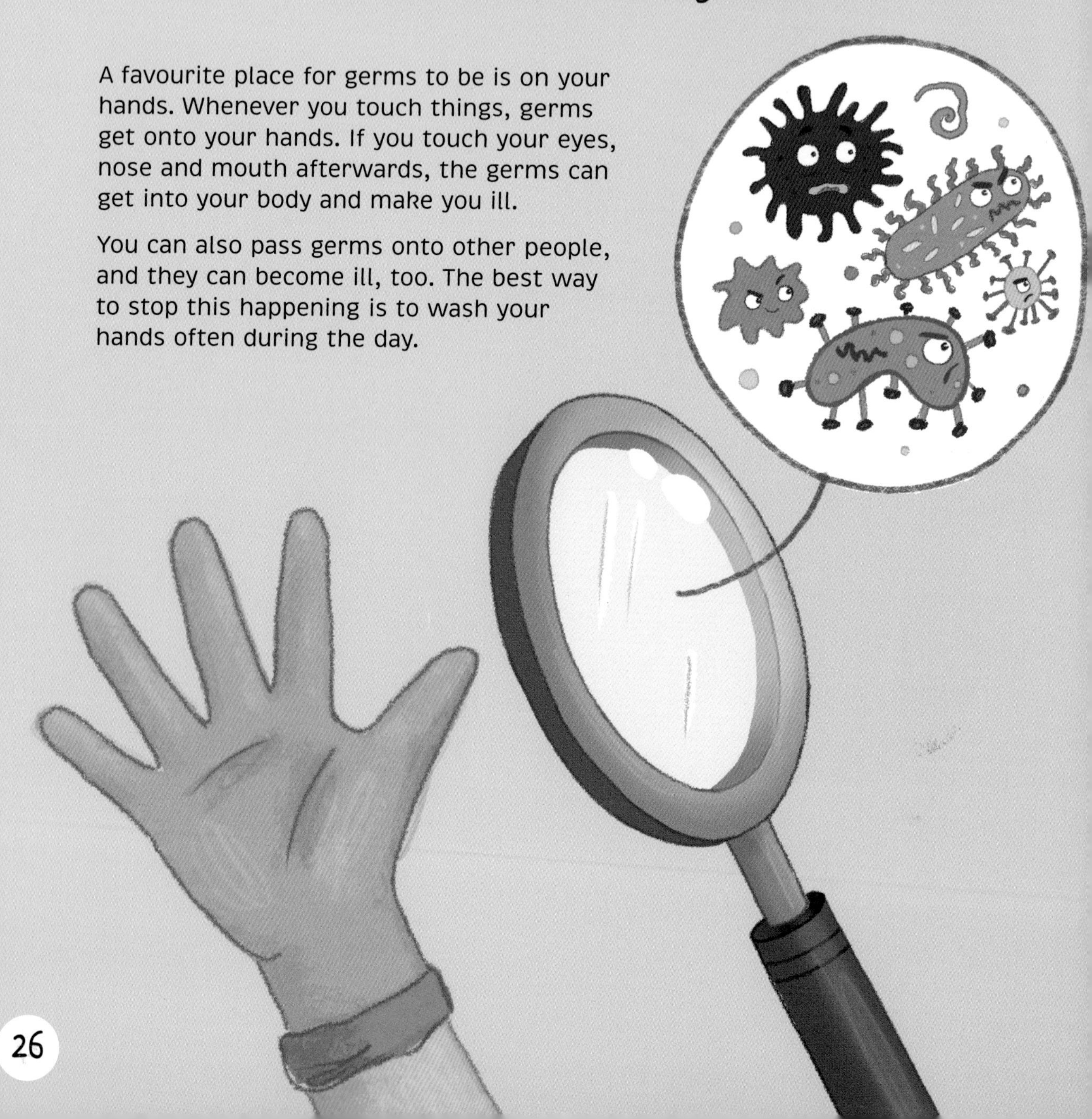

Wash your hands with warm water and soap. Make sure you wash the fronts and backs, and in between your fingers. Don't forget your nails. Wash for as a long as it takes you to sing 'Happy birthday' twice. Then rinse with warm water, and dry your hands.

WASH YOUR HANDS ...

- before and after meals
- after playing outside
- after touching pets
- after going to the toilet
- after coughing or blowing your nose
- after visiting someone who's ill.

LOOKING AFTER YOU

Your body is very precious.

It does so many things for you and makes you who you are.

It's your job to look after your body, and keep it in top condition. That way, it will keep on working hard for you for many years to come.

It's also important to take care of your feelings. Sometimes, things might go wrong. You might find yourself feeling sad, or falling ill. Don't worry, this is completely normal. Looking after yourself can help to stop some of these things from happening.

If you're worried about anything that's happening to your body, make sure you tell someone you trust. Everybody's body needs a bit of help sometimes. So take good care of it and your brilliant body should last you a lifetime!

GLOSSARY

Acid
Chemical in fizzy drinks that can make your teeth rot.

Bacteria
Tiny living things that can be helpful or harmful.

Body odour (BO)
Smell caused by sweat mixing with bacteria on your skin

Calcium
Chemical found in some types of food, such as cheese or milk, that keeps your teeth and bones strong.

Carbohydrates
Types of starchy food, such as bread, potatoes and pasta, that give you energy.

Dairy
Foods that are made from milk, such as butter, cheese and yoghurt.

Energy
Power that makes your body able to do work.

Germ
Bacteria and viruses are both types of germ.

Nutrients
Nourishing parts of food.

Protein
Nutrient found in foods such as vegetables, fish, nuts and eggs.

Recharge
Fill with more energy.

Virus
Tiny living thing that can be harmful.

FIND OUT MORE

Websites

www.bbc.co.uk/bitesize/topics/z9yycdm/articles/zxvkd2p

A website from BBC Bitesize with fun information and quizzes about staying healthy.

www.dkfindout.com/uk/human-body/keeping-healthy/

More information about how to look after your body.

www.healthforkids.co.uk/staying-healthy/

Working with the NHS (National Health Service), this website has facts about maintaining a healthy body and a healthy mind.

Books

Healthy For Life: Food and Eating/Keeping Fit/Self-esteem and Mental Health by Anna Claybourne (Franklin Watts, 2018)

Why Do I Have to: Eat Healthy Food?/Go to Sleep?/ Keep Clean? by Kay Barnham (Franklin Watts, 2021)

INDEX